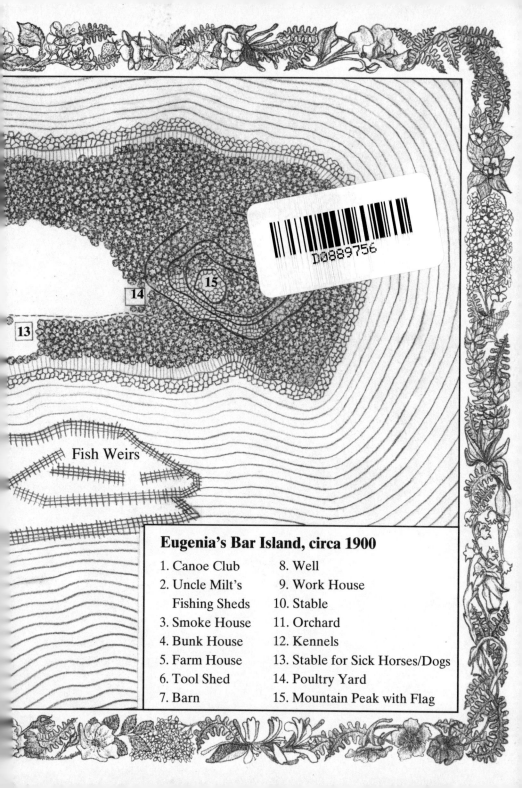

Fish Weirs

Eugenia's Bar Island, circa 1900

1. Canoe Club
2. Uncle Milt's Fishing Sheds
3. Smoke House
4. Bunk House
5. Farm House
6. Tool Shed
7. Barn
8. Well
9. Work House
10. Stable
11. Orchard
12. Kennels
13. Stable for Sick Horses/Dogs
14. Poultry Yard
15. Mountain Peak with Flag

Parasols of Fern

7⁵⁰

Parasols of Fern

A Book About Wonder

written by **Jack Perkins**
illustrated by **Mary Jo Perkins**

with original text from the reminiscences of
Eugenia Rodick

First Edition Published June 1994.

Library of Congress Cataloging-in-Publication Data

Perkins, Jack, 1933-
    Parasols of fern : a book about wonder / written by Jack
Perkins ; illustrated by Mary Jo Perkins ; with original text
from the reminiscences of Eugenia Rodick. — 1st ed.
        p.   cm.
    ISBN 0-934745-17-X : $18.95
    1. Bar Island (Hancock County, Me.) – Social life and
customs.
    I. Perkins, Mary Jo.   II. Rodick, Eugenia.   III. Title.
F27.M9P47   1994
974.1'45–dc20   93-10874
                                                    CIP

The paper herein and the memories printed on it are all recycled.

Printed in the United States of America
10 9 8 7 6 5 4 3 2 1

ACADIA PRESS and the colophon are trademarks of Acadia Publishing Company.

This book is dedicated to
Claire Lambert and Gladys O'Neil,
finders and keepers of memories,
in whose honor a portion of the
proceeds will be donated to:
The Jesup Memorial Library
The Bar Harbor Historical Society.

Foreword

The author will have plenty of chances to be heard herein. The *pre facto* collaborator, Eugenia Rodick, will reveal herself through her years-ago reminiscences. But for the illustrator and the techniques she employed, a brief introduction might serve.

It was she, moved by her reading of Eugenia's childhood memories, who determined to set them with artist's pencil to paper. That was the start of the book.

Exhaustively, she researched the general look of the late 1800's (an 1895 Montgomery Ward catalogue facsimile was a great boon). More specifically, she pored over pictures of the island from old postcards and archived etchings to pinhole camera blurs cemented into a family album in the possession of friends, distant relatives of Eugenia. These showed structures, fish weirs, hay racks, prams and pungs, and in a very few choice shots — people. Together these helped the artist "see" the past. Her "seeing", however, was ambiguous. For whenever she tried to imagine 10-year-old Eugenia with her younger brothers David and Serenus romping the island, she kept seeing her own daughter and two younger sons in playful romps generations later. Consequently, the images she produced should be accepted as loving composites, completely faithful to the spirit of the piece if not to precise physiognomies.

(There was one haunting coincidence during the process of illustration. She had done a drawing of the kids playing with a puppy and a straw hat [page 95]. It was only several months later that she was astonished to discover a photograph of young David, posing with a puppy, and wearing *precisely that hat!* Are coincidences always coincidental?)

For the map that serves as opening endpaper, the artist had to be something of a cartographic detective, cross-referencing the pieces of Eugenia's text where she spoke of this building standing just beyond that one, or a road leading a certain direction past something else, with photographs, none of which showed everthing in the island and many of which didn't show much. Consequently, the "Map of Rodick's Island, Circa 1900" is conjectural though the conjecture, we believe, is well-based.

Finally, there is the matter of Eugenia herself. There is a photograph extant of her taken perhaps a decade after the period of this book but none (that we know of) showing her as a child. This was either a problem or, as the artist chose to accept it, an opportunity for artistic creativity.

She did not know what Eugenia Rodick looked like at ten, but she knew the look of wonder; and that, after all, is what the book is about.

The Wonder of Wonder

This is a story of wonder. The book is small because wonder is best seen small. Try to magnify it, scrutinize and analyze it, and like a butterfly perched on a black-eyed Susan, as you near, it flies. Look quickly. Wonder comes in glimpses.

In this case, the glimpses show lives on a single Maine island — Bar Island, it is called today — as nineteenth rolled to twentieth century. The views are seen through the eyes of a child and when dealing with wonder, what better observer? What better ears to hear playful brothers frolic in summer island grasses, popping sun-warmed strawberries into giggling mouths, then dashing off noisily through a field of riotous flowers? What better eyes in that long-ago time before television to behold in something called a stereopticon viewer scenes as fascinating as any animated monsters or widescreen time-travelers latter day media might concoct? What better idea of justice to acknowledge that the earnest toilings of day were duly rewarded by the welcoming warmth of a living room hearth and the yield of a bountiful kitchen? What better sense of feel to hold the memory of walking on waters full of wiggling fish; sense of smell to catch the smoking of herring, the baking of bread, the perfumes of an aunt's damask roses; sense of taste to savor the doughnut balls, gingerbread and mincemeats? What better mind than a child's to recall how championship dogs and thoroughbred horses were raised on the island, how new hybrids of fruit trees were painstakingly grafted to life, how fleece was spun and knit into garments to ward off ferocious winters; how once, a simple, serene sunset was a prayerful benediction, and a family, bonded by love, was born, grew up, passed on?

At its core, then, this is the simple tale of a girl's playful life and the memories she took from it. But it is more. For there are other glimpses as well, and other glimpsers.

There are a man and a woman from away who, generations after the girl, find the island. Come in search of grownup reality, they discover it in the wisdom of a child whom they never meet but with whom they walk and from whom they learn. That surprises them.

It shouldn't. For the thesis these thin pages proffer is this:

Anyone seeking Great Truths (and isn't it our national intellectual pastime to seek Great Truths?) might ignore the thirty-five thousand books published each year, the 350,000 hours of TV delivered by the average cable system, and the ceaseless scramblings of radio whistling in the ether. Should disregard headlines and the analysts of them, spurn blatherings of monomial talk hosts and ego-starved talk guests, shun subway Socrates and coffee cup Thoreaus, and eschew the rantings of rock and rap. Disdain, in other words, most of the "truths" that daily bombard us, for in those "truths" are scant truth and no wonder.

Instead, let the seeker turn to a child, perhaps, as in our case, a frolicking girl whose life seemed a heaven-blessed medley of love among family, nuzzling puppies, shading bracken fronds, swings under oaks, of manageable chores and memorable play, hardships that were not hard, and days that ended in sunsets that wouldn't.

Are such things of worldly moment? Of course not. But the seeker must understand that our lives are not worldly momentous. Nor should we expect nor want them to be. For as we design our thoughts and actions to "make a difference," "make a living," or "make a mark," we neglect to make a life. Pursuing greatness, plotting power, planning privilege, we dishonor the greatness, power and privilege we have.

To the saying "Life is what happens while we're busy making plans," add a corollary:

Life is what happens — all the little things that

happen — that don't seem important enough to be life.

Whenever our notion of "important" gets that skewed, we desperately need an island.

Islomaniacs

If wonder comes in glimpses, islands are apt. Islands are made for glimpses. Limited themselves, they impose limits upon all who tread them. Not like mainlands where views and perplexities abound so that minds overload. No, on islands perspectives are bounded, and within their harboring boundaries a mind finally can focus on the boundless.

That's why we're here. Why a few years ago a middle-aged man and woman, too long enmeshed in cities and busyness, rung-climbing and tax-planning, took the drastic (to friends, inexplicable) decision to call a halt, to uproot, translocate a nation's breadth from home and there pull snugly about them, like a comforting blanket, the isolation and comprehensibility of a Maine coastal island.

It has to be small, we felt, the island of choice, small enough to walk in an hour, no more. Small enough to be coherent, assimilable. Any bigger is not really an island. (Geographers notwithstanding, Manhattan is not insular; Manhattan notwithstanding, "insular" is no insult.)

When first we discovered the small island that would never be ours though we would call it ours, we were occasional visitors to Maine smitten by the feel of the place and its people and seeking a getaway corner for ourselves.

It was empty. For fifty years, the corner called Bar Island had been uninhabited.

A half mile upthrust of granite, soil and woods, through history it had worn other names, known other lives, welcomed other walkers through its flower-spattered meadow, ripened wild cherries for other eager mouths, spread sublime panoramas of sunglint seas as welcome reward to other climbers of its peak, but as we happened upon it, we knew none of this. Like most discoverers, we preferred to think our discovery unique, our experience unprecedented.

And like most mainlanders drawn to an island, we didn't understand why. What causes "islomania," as Lawrence Durrell chose to call it?

Is there an atavistic impulse imprinted on the human soul to return to the bosom of waters from which first wriggled some distant progenitors?

Is it the echo of Crusoe, of the lore that lies to us twice: first assuring us that self-sufficiency is desirable, then persuading us that it can be had?

Do we take an island as antidote for bigness?

Is it the quest for root in rock that sets us adrift?

All these questions bubbled forth as we navigated our passage, but their answers did not bubble with them. There was much we didn't know. This wasn't a rational process. Never throughout it did we *know* as much as we *felt.* But what we *felt* was that, somehow, *this was right.*

The day we found the island we walked it for only two hours before deciding to purchase; but that impulsive decision *felt right* because impulse, we believed and believe, is how fate's designs are meant to be realized. Spending the next eager months plotting construction of a vacation cabin so far removed we would see it only two, maybe three times a year, *felt right* because vacation change ought to be drastic; closer, more convenient would not be vacation. And, finally, after two years of impatience, taking virgin steps across the new cabin's threshold on a summer's afternoon *felt right* because this "camp," designed by a man who barely knew us, was not just a house, not just a home, but — we knew instantly — our home!

In the second summer of too-rare visits, we came to understand that vacations would no longer suffice, that the woody, airy aerie on Frenchman's Bay was where we should live all the time; family, friends and profession were fixed on another coast; we would be required to leave behind the external obligations and appendices of familiar lives, to turn our world and selves upside down, but even the radicalness of that change *felt at least tentatively right.*

So we did it.

The first queasy months of dislocation, the first winter snowbound alone on our island raised icy crags of doubt, to be sure, but with more determination than confidence we strapped on snowshoes and tromped them all down, and eventually snows did melt, spring did come, and summer and fall, and everything — our lives in this strange and glorious new place, our shrugging into fresh wardrobes of behavior and being—*felt, finally, unarguably right!*

Why? Something in us needed to know why this had happened. As rational people do, we sometimes used rationality to mask or avoid our feelings, but sometimes — this time — to explain them.

We had been seduced. How? What was it about not *all* islands but *this* island? What were its secrets? Where lay its mystical powers to attract?

For anyone, anytime, it is important to know where you are. To fix yourself in place and time, to know your point on the continuum.

This was our point: the first home we had ever chosen. What a rare privilege that is! For once in your life, not your parents, not a commanding officer, not your boss, but *you* choose where you shall live.

This island, by our choice, was ours; we, by fate's choice, were its.

The decision had been intuitive but now we set about to rationalize it. We determined to go to school, as it were, and major in Bar Island; we would come to know intimately this home we had chosen, not just what it was when we found it, but what it had been way back, before even our imaginings.

Fishes and Magma

And Ice a Mile Thick

It was the age of fishes. Seaweed was the highest form of plant life. Primeval seas teemed, and the first adventuresome creatures began to crawl forth onto land, wondering if land might be a nice place to live, for a change.

When was this? Scientists speak of the Pleistocene epoch of geologic time. And the Pliocene, Miocene, Oligocene, Eocene, and Paleocene epochs. This was before those. Before the entire Cenozoic era; prior to the Cretaceous period, the Jurassic and Triassic periods of the Mesozoic era; pre-dating the Permian, Pennsylvanian and Mississippian periods — way back in that part of misty pre-history called the late Devonian period of the Paleozoic era — 375 million years ago — the elemental rock that would be our island was born.

We can't call that proto-land North America because continents were still moving, floating about on the surface of molten earth. Probably the chunk we now call North America had just collided with the crustal plate which would one day divide into Africa and Europe, the titanic collision crumpling our continent's fender so that suddenly (geologically speaking) there were mountains — the Appalachians. Down whose flanks ran rivers which slowly, laboriously tumbled rocks into pebbles, broke pebbles into soil, carried soil back into shallow seas where it grew on sea bottoms as layers of silt, ever thicker, ever heavier, gravel and coarse sand, hundreds of feet thick, pushing down on itself with such pressure that it hardened once more into rock. And that rock, sedimentary and conglomerate, created on ancient sea-beds so many millenia ago, would one day be named by geologists the Bar Harbor Series. The bedrock of our island.

The molten, moving earth, though, still had tricks. Alternately it began to rise and subside. What yesterday was sea bottom, tomorrow was land. Then not. Continents wandered, riding their tectonic plates. Occasionally globs of molten material from earth's deep furnace would force their way up toward the surface. Sometimes to erupt in volcanoes, sometimes fracture the rock of the Bar Harbor series, squeeze through, around and over, and deposit layers of magma which would slowly cool into a hard rock called diorite. Other times to push up, bubbling the crust, and leave huge domes of another especially resistant rock called granite.

Erosion resumed. Soft rock was stripped away, leaving tough granite cores, and those less resilient rocks which happened to be protected by caps of hard diorite. Resisting erosion, these constructions soon towered over surrounding land as mountains, or, when seas returned, as islands.

Such was our island, an upfolding of that sedimentary rock called the Bar Harbor series capped and protected from erosion by diorite. Beside it, a huge core of granite, many times larger, would one day be called Mount Desert Island.

It would take millions and millions of years. And only in the last million would Earth unleash its latest trick: ice. Four times, continental glaciers rumbled down over northern North America. The last began a hundred thousand years ago, reached its height eighteen thousand years ago. Ice a mile thick weighted New England, covering the small island, scraping and scouring it, depressing it, pushing its head once more into the sea. When finally the glacier retreated, melting away, it released so much water that sea levels on the depressed land rose 300 feet above the levels we know today. Half way up hillsides can be found remnants of beaches.

Again, seas subsided, land rebounded, and again there stood the island, its diorite cap upthrust from surrounding waters, the sedimentary rocks of its Bar Harbor series exposed on its flanks below that cap, while ocean waves slowly washed in to dump at the western end of the island an accretion of gravel that would form a bar to lie beneath the water when tides were high but run exposed when waters were low, a bar connecting the small island with the much larger granite island a quarter-mile away. An island off an island, tied together yet separate.

In that kinship the barren island existed for countless centuries. It basked in the sun, bore the waves, received rains and the seeds dropped by birds. From those seeds, sprouted plants. To feed on those plants came animals, insects, reptiles.

And people?

As the island had come late to the face of earth, people came late to the island. It's understandable: the only people on earth at that time were scarce scatterings of stone-age nomads who, having not yet discovered agriculture, were still chipping out stone points to kill animals. This was the age before pottery, before metals, long before any sort of civilization, or alphabet, or numbers, or money. It would be four thousand years until Egyptians would build Pyramids; six thousand before the reign of King Solomon; seven thousand years before Christ.

The island waited.

It Has Always Been Easier To Claim Than Possess

Who discovered the island?

The first people to cross the small land bridge to the island were most likely descendants of the first people to cross the great land bridge to our continent from Siberia 14,000 years ago. Hunters pursuing game they were, those "first Americans", and they found a land only recently uncovered by ice. Slowly but determinedly — and it was one of history's boldest and most epochal migrations — they worked their way the width of the land mass following caribou, musk ox, and woolly mammoths, until 11,000 years ago they hit Maine (though the tree-less plains looked more like Arctic tundra than the Maine we know).

By 5,000 years ago, those first migrant hunters had been either replaced by or evolved into a culture well advanced in its use of tools and techniques, still hunters but also apparently fishermen and boat builders, with distinctive rituals. They buried their dead in cemeteries, and it is from the ochre-colored powder they sprinkled over buried artifacts that today they are popularly known as "Red Paint People." (Archeologists prefer "Maritime Archaic.")

We don't know — probably never will — how the transition occurred between those Red Paint People and what five millenia later would be called Indians. ("Indians" thanks to Columbus, an explorer who not only didn't know where he was going but wasn't sure where he was when he got there.) Europeans egocentrically spoke of their "discovery" of the new world. Indians thought differently. In their belief, Gluskap, the first man on earth, had been created near the very lands we now call Maine. They were his spiritual heirs who would find our small island.

Today, we know them as Abnaki, of the Algonkian language group, of the tribes named Penobscot, Passamaquoddy, Micmac, and Maliseet. Perhaps, at first, they came as summer people, leaving villages inland, packing kids and pets into birch bark canoes to paddle off for summer vacations at the shore. (Such junkets no challenge for their ocean-worthy canoes.) Working vacations they were, men fishing and building birch-bark lodges for the season; women digging and shucking clams, peeling birch bark and plucking sweet grass to make intricate baskets; children playing and enjoying the fruitful bounty of nature's summer. And not just of summer, for there's evidence that these people soon began residing hereabouts in all seasons, taking advantage of autumn's, winter's and spring's bounties as well.

They called the big island *Pemetiq*, meaning "a

range of mountains." Presumably they found names, too, for the small islands alongside the large one, especially the one so closely bound to Pemetiq by the gravel and mussel-shell bar a quarter-mile long uncovering with the tide twice a day. What fascination that phenomenon must have held for them! Did they cross that bar at low tide to explore the little island, gather its mussels, fish from its shores, gather its late summer berries? And maybe, now and then, just play? Well-grassed and amply-treed, the island must have been a fine place to play. Did some, eventually, choose to live there? One archeologist has found signs of a "shell midden," an old Indian refuse heap, on the island.

What early Europeans came by? One persistent historian theorizes that centuries before Christ, crafty Phoenicians sailed their way as far as Maine's Monhegan island, leaving behind an inscription to prove it on the rock of neighboring Manana. He does not claim they got up as far as we're talking, though, so who did? Maybe Norsemen, perhaps British, most likely a Portuguese navigator named Don Estevan Gómez, and assuredly the French explorer, Samuel de Champlain.

Of Champlain's visit, there is precise record. It was on the morning of September 6, 1604 that he sailed by on a 17-ton, square-rigged ketch with twelve sailors and two Indian guides. He passed, ran briefly aground, made notes in his log book, sketched maps, thought up names for places he saw (like the granite dome, Pemetiq, which he saw as an island with bare-topped mountains, *l'Île des Monts Déserts*, later to be anglicized to Mount Desert).

He only sailed by, but that was enough for the French government to lay claim to the whole region. And, years later, for King Louis XIV to grant part of those lands to another Frenchman, a curious fellow with (to us, today) a curiously familiar name. He referred to himself with a title: the *Sieur de Cadillac*.

Now, if Indians were misnamed, it was not their fault. That Cadillac carried a fraudulent moniker was entirely his. In truth, he was a cunning French commoner named Antoine Laumet who figured that only noblemen could amount to anything, so, before journeying to the far lands of America where no one would know him, he made up a phony name and title for himself and for the rest of his life pretended to be of French nobility.

He, too, made the most of a brief visit. At most, he spent one summer around Mount Desert before moving on to found the city of Detroit. Still, centuries later, the highest peak on Mount Desert (indeed the highest on the east coast of the Americas anywhere north of Rio) would be named Cadillac Mountain. And, in Michigan, an automobile would be manufactured bearing not only his self-given name but, on its hood, the bogus coat of arms he had synthesized.

It was in 1688 that King Louis granted to this self-proclaimed *Sieur de Cadillac* vast tracts of the American coast and islands offshore. He now owned these lands, owned the small island, so impressive-looking French documents declared.

But the English were printing their own documents. And sending men, guns and ships to enforce them. For years, English warriors attacked French settlers and forces around the small island. French warships hid behind it, lying in ambush for English vessels sailing by so that ever after the waters would be called Frenchman's Bay. Basically, the French controlled from this point north, the English, from here south. This was the warring place.

After the war, by 1760, the American revolution approached. Those were the days of the patriots, Samuel Adams and John Hancock, struggling with a dream. As that dream's realization neared, the Crown inevitably losing its grasp, Britain's governor for Massachusetts (to which the lands of "the Maine" belonged), Governor Francis Bernard determined to get a piece of paper for himself. He persuaded King George III to grant him a deed to Mount Desert and its adjoining islands.

As fates would have it, the paper did little good because angry colonists, caught up in a revolutionary fever, sent Governor Bernard scurrying back to London, and confiscated his American property.

After the war, his son, John Bernard, who had sided with the patriots rather than father or king, tried to reclaim the lands. But he encountered unique opposition.

The other claimant — to describe her charitably — was a willful and persistent woman. "Simple-minded" and "grasping," said historian Samuel Eliot Morison, less reticent.

Her name was Madame Marie Therese de Gregoire. And who was she? None other than the granddaughter of that sly old pretender, *Sieur de Cadillac*.

In she sailed from France, the Madame, husband and children in tow and armed with high-powered letters of introduction from Benjamin Franklin and Thomas Jefferson, and, most importantly, the Marquis de Lafayette who personified the invaluable support which France had lent the American revolution. So grateful were the patriots to him and any who came in his name that Samuel Adams and John Hancock themselves eagerly led the Massachusetts legislature through some hasty legislative contortions.

In order to own land, Madame de Gregoire and her husband would have to be American citizens. So, in 1787, with one document the legislature conferred citizenship upon them, and with a second, granted immediate title to the eastern half of Mount Desert Island, (the governor's turncoat son, John Bernard, getting only the western half), a stretch of mainland and the islands offshore, including that small island connected to Mount Desert at low tide by the bar.

Bar Island, which she had never seen, belonged to Madame de Gregoire. So said the documents.

Which must have surprised the man who thought *he* owned it.

Mr. Rodick's Island

It was familiar. It was a name we had heard.

In town, in Bar Harbor, we drove a Rodick street. Century-old photographs of town remembered a formidable Rodick House hotel. Indeed, part of the Rodick family, we were told, had once lived on Bar Island.

Our predecessors. Kin to our souls. Drawn, we presumed, by the same allures as we. If that were the case, then to know Bar Island we needed to meet these people named Rodick.

We found them in a basement, where memories belong. "Down cellar" at the little town library, we visited Gladys O'Neil and her Bar Harbor Historical Society. Found records, clippings, and musty, blurred documents that would serve as enciphered introductions.

First, to Daniel Rodick.

The country was young. The first settlers had come to Frenchman's Bay in 1768. The very first, John Hamor and his wife, happily hewed a home near a cove on Mount Desert Island (later called Hulls Cove), but short-lived their happiness would be for he died the next year. Bereft, his widow sent an urgent plea for help to her brother down in Harpswell, Maine, and that brother,

Daniel Rodick, hurried to her side, he and his wife the second family group in the area. A brother-in-law, Elisha Cousins, followed, making three, and that was the nucleus of the new town.

It was still rugged country. As late as 1790, settlers voted bounties on bears, wolves and wildcats. Political offices in incipient towns reflected life's simple realities: Official Surveyor of Shingles, Surveyor of Staves, Sealer of Leather, Culler of Fish, Hog Reeve, and Tithingman. Daniel Rodick was selected official town Fence-Viewer, clearly a man of repute.

Living near the shore in those late 1700's, he must have found himself increasingly fascinated by the small island that lay out there in those waters. What a splendid place that would be to run sheep, to dig clams, and even, he must have conjectured, one day to live. So widely acknowledged was his attachment to the island that, before long, it was commonly deemed, if not deeded, to be his. However designated on official survey maps in far-off Boston, to locals, it was simply "Rodick's Island."

We could picture him of a sunny afternoon, strolling across from the new little town called Eden, over the gravel and mussel-shell bar which receding tides exposed twice a day to the island rising beckoningly from the shrunken waters of Frenchman's Bay. The island was a half mile long, west to east, a quarter-mile north to south. The bar traversed to its western end where a slope rose through woodland to a plateau a hundred feet above. Following the plateau eastward he would have climbed a densely wooded hill to the island's eastern peak, a bare outcropping of rock, of diorite, that from 170 feet above sea level afforded spectacular views all around. Up Frenchman's Bay toward the mainland of Gouldsboro town to the north; across at She Porcupine (later Sheep Porcupine), Burnt Porcupine, Long Porcupine and Bald Porcupine islands to the east (from town the wooded islands appeared as porcupines lying out there, quills poking up in shaggy disarray); to the southeast toward the open stretches of ocean leading everywhere; to the south, back toward Eden and the bare peaks of Mount Desert Island; and to the west and northwest toward Hulls Cove.

By this time, Hulls Cove was where Madame de Gregoire had taken up residence with a singular determination. She had not inveigled both citizenship and land grant from the Massachusetts legislature because she loved the lonely lands but because she wanted to make money; she was Mount Desert's first land speculator. Finding a squatter, or someone laying claim to land that was hers, she happily sold him (for milled gold) what he thought he already owned. It was just such a deal she offered in turn to Daniel Rodick and he accepted. The purchase price has been lost but if she charged him what she charged others, the foresighted Mr. Rodick, in 1792, bought Bar Island for five dollars!

A few years later, he deeded half of it over to his third son, David, who built upon it a small house for his wife and growing family.

During the War of 1812, once more, if but briefly, the island was called on to serve. Two fishermen, William Mason and Thomas Paine, were out in a small boat in Frenchman's Bay one day when overrun and fired upon by the crew of a marauding English ship. Mason was mortally wounded. Paine managed to get the wrecked boat to Rodick's Island where Mason was lifted ashore, given emergency treatment, but died the next day — in the Rodick's new house.

New home. David Rodick would live there his whole life, then this third son would bequeath the place to his own third son, David, Jr., who, in his time, would pass it to a daughter named Flora.

The small island, which over millenia had been variously an unknown geologic accretion of rock, host to the mysterious Red Paint People, happy fishing ground for summering Abnakis, shelter for hide-and-seek French and English naval warriors, and an almost overlooked tidbit of real estate lumped into far larger land dealings — this place, Rodick's Island/Bar Island was transformed into that most precious of parcels: a family's home!

Lilies By A Cellar Hole

Names and dates, decedents and heirs — these weren't enough. What were lives like on the island? This vital part of the story still eluded us.

Each day, wandering, we wondered. Where had the Rodick house stood? At two spots on the island we found ruins, fragments of foundations, one of rock at the site of our own home; another, a hundred yards distant, more recent, of concrete. Neither was it.

Old pictures showed the home, stately and exalted, surmounting a hill toward the western end of the island, beyond the meadow, perhaps in what now was woods. No one could tell us. The guardian of the town's memory didn't know. A writer and researcher of area history had looked, hadn't found. So we set it our task. Our first step toward understanding the lives that had preceded ours was to locate the Rodick homesite.

It took many days till we came on a clue. One afternoon, deep in the forest, behind a curtain of dense spruce, in mottled light filtering down through a canopy of popple and oak, we found day lilies! Not flowers to spring wild from nature, day lilies, but dooryard flowers, clear signs that at some point past, people had lived near. This had to be it.

It was. So fast beneath low-lying branches we would never have found it. Only patches of tumbled gray rocks, but geometrically aligned, architectural. All that remained of the Rodick's old cellar.

Nearby, lilies of the valley. And ancient lilac bushes, grown to twenty feet high, still burgeoning each spring.

Out in the meadow, a stooped platoon of valiant trees, vestiges of the Rodick's orchard, still struggled against their own deaths to produce life. In autumn we could pluck their wizened fruit, too sour to eat out of hand but worth saucing.

Did the Rodicks make sauce? What did they do with their island lives? Photographs, clippings, engravings couldn't tell us. We needed not statistics but the texture and tone of beings. To know yourselves, you must know those who preceded you. Not an original thought.

Cicero: *"To be ignorant of what happened before you were born, is to be ever a child. For what is man's lifetime unless the memory of events is woven with those of earlier times?"*

In Cicero's counsel, though, was a subtle paradox. While not wanting to be "ever a child," we did yearn for childness, for the child's innocent appreciation. At the same time, though, we craved the adult's understanding of context, of what is, which can only be measured by knowledge of what was.

Well, the advantage of being an adult, if one does it right, is being able to choose. A child can be only a child. An adult, as moods change, can be either.

As adults, we searched. And, appropriately, when we found what we sought it was in the mind of a child.

Meeting Eugenia

Eugenia Rodick. Great-great grandaughter of Daniel who back in 1770 first fell under the thrall of the island; great grandaughter of David who built the house and started the dynasty; grandaughter of David, Jr. who added to both.

As a child in the last years of the nineteenth century, Eugenia romped the island's meadow and plucked its fruits, tucking away, all the while, sweet green memories. She waited till grown and married before recording her childhood recollections. Not until 1938 did Eugenia Rodick Martin sit before a typewriter to transfer years-ago images to paper, then, work done, put paper away.

It would be another forty years before someone — we don't know who but perhaps an heir going through her memorabilia — happened upon the slender typescript and decided it should not be allowed to be lost, disposed with other flotsam of a life as belongings were dispersed. Maybe that's how it happened. Anyhow, one day, unheralded, an envelope arrived at the little Jesup Memorial Library in Bar Harbor. In it, with scant explanation, were those typewritten pages — precious shards of a childhood three quarters of a century earlier.

The pages were duly recorded and again filed away, for more years to go mostly unread. People didn't seem interested in other people's memories — too busy making their own.

We were interested. When Jesup's librarian presented the slender pages, we read hungrily. From Eugenia's words, we gleaned glimpses, heard whispers and hints of the essence of lives in a time and place both simpler and more complex.

She began slowly, drily, as though needing to prime memories with data. This was Eugenia the adult, withdrawing as adults do when confronting new people or new thoughts to the familiarly prosaic. Discuss weather, recite statistics.

Eugenia remembers

"One hundred and fifty acres..."

Bar Island lies in the harbor of Frenchman's Bay, one-quarter mile north of Bar Harbor. An island of one hundred and fifty acres of pasture and woodland, it rises abruptly from the ocean about one hundred feet to a cleared plateau.

At the eastern end is a densely wooded hill.

At the western side of the island, however, we find its most distinctive feature. There, at the foot of the slope, lies a little patch of level land which runs in a southerly direction, sometimes underwater, sometimes exposed, a gravel bar to Bar Harbor. The bar is hard gravel on top but runs off to mussel beds and clam flats at its extreme edges. It varies in width from 100 to 1000 feet. From half-tide to half-tide, where the range from mean low to mean high is 12 feet, this bar forms a roadway making it possible to walk or drive to Bar Harbor.

What a haven for a sea-faring man who wished

to settle! Here Grandfather Rodick could live surrounded by the sea which he loved and yet be in close touch with his fellow men!

In our grandfather's early days, Bar Harbor had not yet developed as a world famous summer resort. The beauty and charm which later would captivate so many rich and famous people was hidden away in a little fishing hamlet, leaving its mark only on the souls and hearts of the few inhabitants, most of whom followed the sea for a livelihood.

As at Nantucket, hardly a household was without some souvenir of the long voyages to the Orient, South America or the Indies. Those who did not go down to the sea on long voyages got their living from the sea in other ways.

At first, Grandfather had a fishing business on the island. He built large weirs to catch herring, for those were the days when the big fishing boats bound

for the Grand and Georgian Banks put in to Bar Harbor to buy barrel after barrel of herring for bait.

When fish were running, a flag was raised on the tall flag pole which was located on a high part of the island, a signal to the fishermen passing up and down the coast.

The bait had to be iced as did the fish caught on the Banks so Grandfather went into the ice

business. Winters were long and cold and a large crew of men were employed to cut ice at Witch Hole Pond and at Eagle Lake. Then there was the long haul on sledges to the ice houses in Bar Harbor. These were located on the shore opposite Bar Island and here the big blocks of ice were stored in sawdust to await the calls of the fishermen.

Also, big fish houses were built on the shore at Bar Island and large racks of fish were dried and salted, and in the smoke house long strings of herring were smoked. These fish found a ready market.

When, finally, Bar Harbor began to develop as a summer resort, Grandfather Rodick had the money to build two large cottages in Bar Harbor where he took in summer boarders and gave employment to many people on Mount Desert Island.

First, The Artists

We knew what had become of those cottages; we had read of Bar Harbor's metamorphosis.

It had started with Thomas Cole, forerunner of that cluster of American painters to be called the Hudson River School, artists who found their inspiration not in mythology nor the feminine figure but in America's landscape.

Cole came for the first time to Mount Desert in September, 1844, travelling eight days overland from Castine to stay at a farmhouse at Schooner Head, to sketch, then go home and rave. That started it.

Others followed. Their paintings, taken home, showed the social elite of the cities that at Mount Desert awaited great beauty if they could but afford to get here.

They could. A prominent New York lawyer, inspired by the paintings of Mount Desert by Cole colleague Frederick Church, one summer's day landed at Southwest Harbor with wife, children *and piano*. By wagon and sailboat they slowly made their way to Albert Somes' tavern at Somesville for a summer's vacation.

More artists came.

In 1883, the painter David Maitland Armstrong set up his easel on the shore at Bar Harbor looking northward and onto canvas meticulously laid irridescent oils. There was the bar, stretching at low tide toward Bar Island; there were geese waddling along the bar, a woman and children strolling; to either side, the Rodick's herring weirs, brush fences in the water; fishermen pulling a rowboat onto the bar; over on the island, a fishing schooner hauled up for bait; three white buildings, part of the fishing operation; and up the hill on the crest of the island, a small but stately white house, the Rodick home, the smoke of its chimney curling desultorily into a cerulean and ochre sky.

In the last decades of the nineteenth century this painting was shown throughout the east, enticing yet more visitors to seek out Bar Harbor.

Few turned to dozens; dozens became hundreds, and that was why David Rodick Jr. built first two cottages to house the "rusticators," as they liked to call themselves. And why he soon realized that those guest houses were not enough and began building a hotel in downtown Bar Harbor, coming over from that home on Bar Island each day to follow its progress, until, in 1882, that hotel, The Rodick House, set in truly "fashionable Bar Harbor" on "exclusive Mount Desert Island," had grown to be the largest hotel in New England, largest summer hotel, it was said, in the entire nation! Four hundred guest rooms, a grand ballroom with dances twice a week, dining room, a piazza 500 feet long, and a large lobby renowned as "The Fish Pond" where courtly young men trolled for modest young women. All of that — sumptuous accomodations for up to six hundred guests, but not one private bath! Is it surprising that after only a few years, the famous Rodick House foundered?

Anyway, the wealthy socialites who were Bar Harbor's summer people in those days, had already had enough rusticating and begun building their own magnificent mansions, each more opulent, with more extravagant fittings and fixtures than the next, and all of them — in that delicious reverse snobbery of the era — called "Cottages."

There was Joseph Pulitzer running his newspaper empire in summer and fall from his great granite structure called Chatwold and trying, in vain, to silence the foghorn at Egg Rock lighthouse whose baying bothered him mightily.

There was J. P. Morgan, more successful wielding clout. Since his drinks kept spilling as he dallied over preprandial cocktails aboard his yacht *Corsair* in the chop of Frenchman's Bay, he cajoled/bullied the federal government into constructing a breakwater at the harbor's entrance to smooth the waters.

There was Morgan's son-in-law, William Pierson Hamilton, so annoyed by the way local papers covered his dinner parties in their society pages that he spent a million dollars to start his own paper.

There were the Stotesburys, he an investment banker from Philadelphia, she a spender of limitless appetite. Purchasing an existing mansion, she immediately set about massive remodeling at a cost of more than one million dollars, creating an eighty room "cottage" with a thirty room servants' wing. She had the whole place — Wingwood House — roofed with imported orange tile but, at her first soiree thereafter, overheard a guest say how "garish" the roof was, so the next morning, first thing, the workmen were back, at her command, re-roofing. Stotesbury stories were legion: the half million dollar safari to kill alligators for a new set of luggage; the gardeners instructed to move the plants around the yard twice a week; the gold fixtures in her bathroom justified with her remark that "they save polishing, you know." History reports that Mr. Stotesbury lived till he was ninety and — should this surprise us? — worked every day.

Opulence and extravagance, Vanderbilts, Blairs, Blaines, Fords, Rockefellers, Morgans, McCormicks, society fetes and social climbers — these were Bar

Harbor at the turning of the century.

But just across the bar, what a totally different life could be found. On the little island, so near, so far.

As we returned to Eugenia's tale, it was a different voice we heard from the proper adult of the preamble. The words still followed one another in stately procession — such was the proper cadence of the day — but within them were glowings of rapture, excitement and wonder. This was Eugenia the child.

Eugenia remembers

"What memories it conjures..."

From the shore, the house was reached by a road winding up the hill. A Cape Cod style house with an ell, it stood foursquare at the top of the slope.

Very high, four steps from the road then a sloping walk and four or five more steps up to the door. Lilac bushes ran down the bank from the top of the steps to the road. Nearer the house were the damask rose bushes, covered at the end of June with spicy rose-colored blooms with the odor of a sweet fresh potpourri.

A great grove of beech and oak and moosewood which ran along the entire northern side of the island encroached on the house from this side and made it impossible to grow anything here except ferns and lilies of the valley.

My recollection of Bar Island is as it was in the

first years of the twentieth century. By this time, the character of Bar Harbor had completely changed: it had become a cottage resort and the Rodick House, occupying the most important site in Bar Harbor, had closed for lack of patronage.

Our Grandfather, David Rodick Jr., had long since been gathered to his fathers!

His youngest daughter, our Aunt Flo, with her husband Charles Pineo, a lawyer, lived in the house and managed the affairs of the family on Bar Island. The farm, the woodlots, the kennels, stables, gardens and household — which was a large one — were all supervised by our Aunt.

The front door was used only for company, and we always stayed in the carriage till it drove around to the back door which was really on the side of the ell. Then my brothers and I would scramble down over the big wheels and into the kitchen.

That kitchen! What memories it conjures up!

Summer, when the garden was at its height, was a busy time in the kitchen. Big pans of peas, beans, corn – later, apples – and all the other garden products were brought in every day to be canned, preserved, pickled or salted according to the custom of the day.

There was always a strapping hired girl and often her husband was one of the hired men. Hired girls were up with the lark and worked till long after dark but always seemed contented and cheerful and ready to make tiny biscuits and doughnut balls for hungry young mouths.

In fall, when the pigs were killed, there was much work disposing of all the meat. In winter, usually some member of the family went deer hunting and often there was a deer hanging in the shed waiting to be cut into steaks and roasts and made into luscious mince meat.

All the year around, there was the milk to take

care of twice a day, churning twice a week, chickens

and ducks to be picked and cleaned for Sunday din-

ners, beans and brown bread for Saturday night and

Sunday mornings, hot bread at least twice a day, clam

chowder, clam pies, bird stews and dumplings,

stripped fish with baked potatoes, salt pork scraps fried

out crisp and brown, mush and milk, fish hash, and

hot spicy gingerbread. Ah!!!

Still, with all that work going on, at the other
end of the kitchen we would usually find old Royal
Young, sitting on one side of the chimney with his curly
head bent over a cane he was carving; and on the other,
Uncle Ed Brewer, just sitting, smoking the inevitable
and awful pipe.

Next to the kitchen and pantry was the dining room with another large pantry at one side. Steep enclosed stairs ran from the dining room up to the second story.

Beyond the hall was the parlor. There stood an organ, and — most fun for us kids — the stereopticon viewer and pictures. Those were magical.

The living room had a large bay window which looked out on the western bay. Here were the slippery, haircloth sofa and chairs, and also a few very comfortable chairs, good reading lights, and several round tables covered with long chenille tablecloths which hung down almost to the floor. These tables were heaped up with books and magazines in ever-growing piles. Country Gentlemen, Harpers, and Scribners are some of the many magazines I remember seeing there. My Uncle, who raised pedigreed pointers and bred race horses, read the horse and kennel magazines religiously.

My Aunt loved flowers and kept up with all that was new in the agricultural world by means of magazines.

Eugenia remembers

"Her results from heaven..."

Flowers grew and flourished for my Aunt as I have never seen them do for anyone else, yet aside from the usual tight bunch on the dining room table in summer I never remember seeing any flowers in the house; plants in abundance, but no arrangements. She had no formal garden nor did she plant any set beds.

But on the left side of the old road beyond the tool house were the sweet peas, my Aunt's pride and joy. Row upon row of them there were, a long line of each color, the vines so high and the brush so thick that we could not see each other from one row to the next. The flowers were cut in the late afternoon and put in water in the old dirt cellar.

Next morning they were delivered to Mr. Moses, the florist in Bar Harbor.

Cross-eyed old Royal Young, the hired man, honest and faithful, made a picture as he went through the streets clad in overalls, toeing out at an angle I have never seen equaled, carrying great baskets of these fragrant, colorful flowers.

Just beside the kitchen door were the pansies lifting up their lovely faces to all who passed.

Around the edges of the open grass plot were masses of peonies, tiger lilies, sweet william, phlox, lupine, columbine, bleeding heart, rambler roses, nasturtiums, and, against the barn, a great mass of golden glow.

Then there were the wild violets, a mass of the loveliest, long, thick-stemmed violets I have ever seen growing wild. There they were, year after year, and we nearly went mad picking them.

Not far from the swings was the family burial ground, a plot enclosed by a picket fence and banked by lilacs, rose bushes and honeysuckle.

When one realizes that nearly all the flowers were in bloom at the same time it gives some conception of the riot of color it presented. What a gorgeous impression for us as children, our swings on the oak trees at the edge of the woods overlooking the garden!

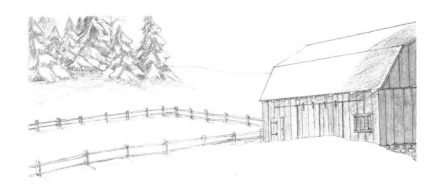

Summer and winter, water had to be hauled
from a well in a big cleared field to the house, barns
and kennels, which meant that on winter mornings
after a snow storm the hired man was up early and out
with the small snow plow to clear the roads both to the
well and down the hill to the bar.

The pasture was behind the big red barn near the swings and on Sundays, the horses — Nancy, the gray mare work horse; Fencer, the driving horse which took us back and forth to town; Molly, my Uncle's trotting horse; and Racquet, a quarter-horse which we used for our very own — stood with their heads on the pasture bars watching us at play.

The kennels housed about 200 dogs whose pedigrees were known all over the country. The champion, young Rip Rap, was at stud and I am told that he is the ancestor of practically every field champion of today in this country.

Personally, I was always somewhat awed by the dogs in the kennel for they barked furiously and jumped on the wire sides of the yards in a most terrifying manner. To me, the one redeeming feature was the puppies who were entrancing when they were big enough to tumble about by themselves.

An old grass road ran between the work house and the old yellow stable opposite, down to the poultry yards which lay at the edge of the pine grove just at the foot of the mountain. On the right hand side of this road was the yellow stable where the mother dogs and sick dogs were cared for.

And next came the orchard. Here in the very earliest days my Aunt, with the help of the hired men, experimented with grafts on the old trees, getting her instruction from garden books — and her results from heaven!

Eugenia remembers

"...how blissfully happy..."

In the center of the island and sloping south was
a big field where the hay was cut. Here, on summer
days, we ran after the mower picking up the hot, wild
strawberries and
watching for birds'
nests occasionally
exposed. When the
hay racks were filled
to overflowing, we
rode in triumph back

to the big, sweet smelling barn and waited for the hay
to be stored in the lofts, all the while watching the
ceaseless flight of swallows in and out, in and out, over
our heads.

All along the steep southern bank of the island grew chokecherry bushes, lovely in bloom in the spring and fun to eat, to pucker up one's mouth in the early fall.

Certainly all the necessities and many of the luxuries of life came from the land and from the waters of the surrounding sea, thus making Bar Island practically a self-sustaining community.

Beyond the sweet peas was the vegetable garden — beans, peas, potatoes, squash, corn, lettuce, pumpkins, beets, carrots and tomatoes.

In the earlier days, spinning and weaving were done at Bar Island. Sheep were kept on Sheep Porcupine, a nearby island, and the wool was made into yarn and cloth. In the early years of the century, my Aunt still knit all the stockings and mittens.

At low tide there was an inexhaustible supply of clams to be dug along the shore and at the edges of the bar.

Uncle Milt now ran the fishing business on the shore. He and his men lived in a small cottage beside the huge fish house which was two stories high and probably 60 by 200 feet. A small car ran on a track from the ocean into one end of this building on the ground level. There were huge racks used in drying the fish and at one end were the smoke pots; prevailing winds had been taken into consideration and various outlets through the building were made so that proper draughts and smoke circulations could be maintained.

The fish were taken fresh and strung through the gills and mouths on stringers three and four feet long and then strapped on racks in the smoke house.

We were always on hand when the fish were running well and it was not an unusual thing for the weirs to be so full that when the seine boats went in to gather the fish we would get out of the boat and wallow around on the solidly packed but live and squirming fish.

In summer, a favorite pursuit was to spear flounders in the puddle made by the dam at the weir. The water was clear and still and we, with our sharp young eyes, quickly picked out the flat shapes of the fish even though nature had given them such excellent camouflage. The game was to spear them between the eyes, for the head was cut off anyway, and this left the fillets in perfect condition. It was but a second's work to impale them on our spears and in no time at all we had a pail full of fresh fish for dinner.

We were usually wet and bedraggled but how blissfully happy on those summer days!

Eugenia remembers

"It was not always convenient ..."

It was not always convenient to live at Bar Island for the well-known reason that time and tide wait for no man. Even in the days when life was lived at a more leisurely pace, we could not always wait for the tide and sometimes drove either to or from the island before the tide had ebbed sufficiently to uncover the bar.

Many times, I remember the water seeping into the bottom of the high carriage and the horse having to swim for a few feet in the low spots. Even more exciting it was to gallop across when the tide was rising and we wondered if we could make the other side.

Many times, my brothers and I were overcome by the urge to go over to the island when the tide was high.

Nothing daunted, we would go down to the foot of the bar at Bridge Street and start to yell for Uncle Milt to come for us in a boat. When I say yell, I mean yell, for sometimes all the men were busy in the fish house and the distance to the island from where we were was about a quarter of a mile, but I can truly say, in tribute to our Uncle's kindness to us and his patience with us, that, once heard, no matter how busy he was, we were not kept waiting long. He or one of his men would row over in a dory, row in that effortless way that fishermen have, without stirring the water, and by the time

they came near the shore we were so eager that we

usually got our feet wet rushing into the boat before it

got to the land.

In winter, in place of the high carriage, a pung
was used to drive to town. This was a sort of low sled
with a driver's seat and a space at the back in which, if
the party were large, seats could be placed, but when
used for hauling supplies, milk, water, etc., a layer of
straw was spread on the floor. This vehicle, unlike
most pungs, had wooden runners because the steel ones
generally used could not stand the wear and tear of
crossing the bar which was, of course, bare the year
around.

Sometimes, in winter, Uncle Milt and his companion, Morris Higgins, would go for a day's shooting at Bald Rock. Just before nightfall of a cold winter day, when there was salt water ice along the shore and a green ocean was whipped to froth by a cold East wind, we would go to the hot, steamy cottage to await their return. Here we stood with our noses against the window until, at last, the boat came in sight. Then we fairly flew down to the water, remembering, however, to avoid the line of slippery rocks where the dish water was thrown out.

The men stood up in the boat which was half full of sea birds, heroic figures in that gray-green light, with the great bulk of their clothes and the guns they carried! They first handed us their guns and then threw the birds ashore. Certainly we never questioned that a generous share belonged to us. Someone tied the birds together by the feet and we went home with all we could carry, the makings of the best dish I know — "Bird Stew."

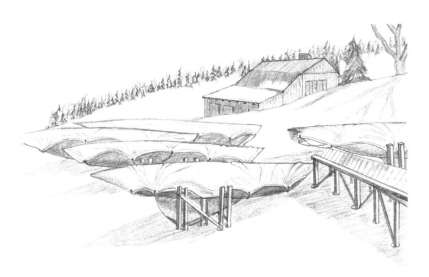

In later years, when yachting became fashionable and the fishing business declined, Uncle Milt used to take care of boats in the winter. They were hauled up along greased ways to cradles and boarded up for the winter; there was often a long row of these boats on the shore. In summer, the yards held 65-foot racing

"knockabouts" which were hauled out of water and cleaned and polished before each weekly race.

All this busy life was carried on at the shore on the small strip of level land from which the bar emerges.

Eugenia remembers

"... it was quite an adventure."

On the island's northern side stood the old Canoe Club. We loved to picnic on the high porch of the now deserted club, where the gulls came to perch and look at us with beady black eyes, waiting for the remains of the lunch. Under the house, at low tide, we gathered starfish and sea urchins.

The Canoe Club had been used for dances and parties and served as headquarters for canoeing which had been a very popular sport. Several Indians had been employed as teachers and it was generally a *flourishing establishment built on land loaned by the family.*

One year I remember when the British and American war ships held a carnival in the harbor, several of the floats were built on the island by sailors from the various ships. These were gorgeous creations and the whole thing a most exciting event for us.

The eastern end of the island, facing the Atlantic Ocean, towered over all with its densely wooded hill which we called "the mountain." It rose directly from

the steep rocky shore. *Fir and pine lay thick on these slopes, beaten on by the cold east wind and the salt spray of winter storms.*

It was quite an adventure to go to the eastern side for it was always dark and damp in the woods and it seemed a long way back to the house. There was a wonderful reward, however, for this venturesome enterprise: a view of the harbor and islands and the magnificent and eternal hills of Mount Desert which, even as children, subdued and impressed us with its rugged beauty.

View of Bar Harbor from Bar Island (circa 1886)

Then there was the western point, a contrast to the boisterous eastern shore. Sometimes on summer evenings, our Aunt would suggest a walk to the point to see the sunset.

A path led through the woods from the back of the house. There were bunchberries, blueberries, partridge berries, checker berries, twin sisters, wild lily of the valley, and trillium and Indian pipe. But best of all, there were ferns of many kinds including wonderfully tall green bracken which we children used for parasols. We promenaded proudly beneath them, emerging finally from the woods to the rocky shore.

Here, we looked across to the spot where Daniel Rodick, our great-great grandfather had first settled at Hull's Cove, and, all unconsciously, gave thanks for the glory and the peace and the benediction of a Maine sunset.

Changes

That was it. No plot, character development, conflict or denouement. Just Eugenia the adult looking once more through the eyes of Eugenia the child, catching glimpses of wonder, tying ribbon around them and tucking them away — a gift for us to unwrap fifty years later.

Fifty years after she set down her tale!

Ninety years after she lived it!

Two centuries after her great-great grandfather had fallen in love with the island!

Much has changed:

The Rodick family has long since departed. The homestead, "foursquare atop the slope," once bubbling with love and keen interests, is gone. Aunt Flora died in 1926. Uncle Charles, Judge Pineo, had the old house jacked up and logrolled toward the island's southeast corner. There it stood till he died. In the forties, unable to maintain it, his heirs afforded it the dignity of being properly torn down instead of vandalized to ruin. Today, just its foundation walls remain, a forlorn cellar hole which visitors to the island, walking on what we call Pineo path, see but don't understand.

To the east of the original homesite, where the old

barn welcomed swooping swallows and wagonfuls of gay children, the rectangular outline of its walls is still traced in the colors of grass. The earthen ramp that led to the barn door is grown over but discernible.

The hay field is a meadow but won't be for long; wild rose and its cousins, blackberry and raspberry, creep. Impermanence is one lesson here.

The trees of the orchard, Aunt Flo's proud hybrids — *"her instruction from garden books and her results from heaven!"* — unpruned and unfertilized for years, bear fruit that is shrunken and sour—but they try. Some tree trunks are gutted by bugs or disease, are hollow and wizened, branches draped with lichen and moss, but still they manage to burst a few perfumed blossoms from branches each spring and set sparse fruit each summer. Persistence is another.

Down by the shore, we find scant sign of Uncle Milt's fishing operation, the smokehouse, tracks, weirs, bunkrooms. No one rows off for a day of birding, nor — mercifully — cooks bird stews. Lobsters are taken in traps offshore but cannot be shoveled up from the bar at low tide (if they could, would anyone prize them?), nor are wriggling fish thick enough to walk on. Mussels abound but mostly are left to the gulls, the Bonapartes, Herrings,

Laughings, and Black-backs, who pry them loose, ascend twenty feet and dash them to rocks below to break them open.

David Maitland Armstrong's painting laid with irridescent oils, titled "The Bar, Bar Harbor, Mt. Desert, 1883" hangs in the Milwaukee Art Museum. Prints sell in Bar Harbor.

The town's "cottage era," its golden age of social gamesmanship, was first staggered by income taxes then razed by wildfires in 1947; only a few mansions remain, one sold for a dollar to the charitable Seacoast Mission, another serving as administration building for College of the Atlantic.

In a small graveyard behind a motel in Hulls Cove, a rough rock is etched with the words "de Gregoire." Virtually no one remembers the Madame is buried there. No town bears her name.

Few remember that Bar Island was once called Rodick's.

Much remains the same:

People still can't agree how to pronounce the Anglicized French name of the big island: is it Mount

De-SERT or Mount DES-ert?

The Eden which artist Thomas Cole found and painted a hundred-fifty years ago is a paradise still. Millions visit each year, Cadillacs mounting Cadillac.

On the small island, though the Rodicks are gone, there is now, as then, a home full of love. There are superficial differences: no longer a stereopticon viewer; instead of *Scribner's* and *Country Gentleman*, *Harrowsmith* and *Country Journal*; two dogs bound, not two hundred. But outside, in the dooryard, remnants of Aunt Flo's beloved day lilies, transplanted, flourish as welcome reminders.

Hiking, today's islanders stop at a chokecherry bush, as Eugenia did, to admire blossoms in spring, to let fruits pucker mouths in autumn. They delight in unearthing rockworks that must have been foundations of kennels or coops.

They hauled a driftwood pole up the peak and there, on holidays, is unfurled a star-spangled banner where, once, the Rodick's signal flag beckoned fishermen to bait. They, too, find "wonderful reward" for each climb — the vista laid before them, the "magnificent and eternal hills" which "subdued and impressed" a child decades earlier and have lost not a whit of their power.

Time and tide still don't wait, so passages are carefully timed (a Jeep, today's pung) but still, on occasion, they get caught. In summer, kayaks afford pleasant traverses, but in the thrall of a winter Nor'easter, one is better advised to stay put.

Some visitors to the island, oblivious of tides, or expecting tide of only a foot, get stranded and holler for help. It is a privilege to be "Uncle Milt."

A few things that might have changed, fortunately didn't:

In 1909, someone proposed a causeway and bridge to connect island to town. The town seemed about to approve the construction when the earlier mentioned gentleman of wealth with the wife who gloried in spending it — Mr. Stotesbury — quietly bought up the western end of Bar Island and declared No Bridge!

Someone else plotted to subdivide the island into sixty-six lots. The paper plans still exist, plans that failed. Sometimes the best news is what does not happen.

Such was the case of the stingy millionaire. John D. Rockefeller Jr. purchased the western half of the island from Mr. Stotesbury and, in 1945, resold it for one dollar to Acadia National Park of which he was already the most generous benefactor. A few years later, he tried to buy the eastern end too. Logging teams had moved in, camping on the island, harvesting timber to be floated down to Bucksport with tides for logs and pulpwood. Indeed, not only harvesting, clear-cutting, a practice Mr. Rockefeller found aesthetically and environmentally abhorrent. He sent his agent to the owner with an offer to buy. At first the owner agreed, then, discovering the identity of the potential buyer, greedily raised his price by five hundred dollars. Mr. Rockefeller could surely afford it but refused to be gouged. He withdrew. The island's eastern end remained private.

Else we wouldn't be here.

In 1985, congress drew permanent boundaries for Acadia National Park and Bar Island was inside the line. Private property could remain as in-holdings but no further development would be permitted. The island, so long home to just one family, will never know more. Never, at least, in what most of us consider foreseeable future.

But in the geologic future, will everything change?

The island is a rare place on earth where the record of ages is not buried beneath soil and city but exposed. On its southeast face, cleaved meaningfully, we can see the tilted layers of siltstone called the Bar Harbor Series, the cemented sea-bottom sediments of 400 million years ago. See, too, the protective cap of diorite, the molten magma of the Devonian period, which today is popularly described as "unerodible".

Geologists, though, instruct that diorite is not unerodible. That the lichens we admire as we walk the coast, the yellow or black scabs on shore rock, microscopic pairings of fungus and alga which appear to be harmlessly decorative, in fact are destructive. Given time — geologic time — the acids released by those minuscule organisms will break down the minerals, leaving rock vulnerable to the prying of freezes and roots, and to rains and waves before whose relentless batterings, ultimately, it will succumb. Rock will once more become soil and wash to the bottom of the sea — to start over.

Other forces, too, conspire. World climate warms. Obedient to laws of physics, warming waters expand, seas rise. Small glaciers and ice sheets retreat, adding waters. Looking at the great West Antarctic Ice Sheet, scientists wonder will it, one day, collapse, raising oceans even higher? They realize that northern North America, having rebounded from glaciation, today is subsiding again and the rate of subsidence is quickening.

Land subsides, rock erodes, waters rise, scientists ponder.

This island — Eugenia's island — may feel many footfalls and know countless lives in the meantime, but geologists believe that its destiny, ineluctable, is again to be swallowed by sea. They predict that this summertime musseling place for the painted people of pre-history, this one-time witness to war, this object of international conniving, this *"haven for a sea-faring man who wished to live ... surrounded by the sea which he loved and yet be in close touch with his fellow men"*, this remembered paradise where a child would stroll in the dappled shade of a bracken frond admiring upturned pansy faces, hungering for clam pies and mush, and gathering memories that would resonate through generations, will one day cease to be.

That's what geologists say, but geologists talk epochs and eras.

The rest of us think lifetimes. And by human perspective, the rock that safeguards the island is unerodible enough. For us, the island *is* eternal. And a small girl's memories of joy, everlasting.

The Parasol Lesson

They were commonplace moments she lived but she put them in words and that made the difference. Her words serve as lenses, to magnify the prosaic and render it rare. Children have that knack.

Most adults forget they should try.

Essayist E. B. White didn't forget. On moving to Maine he found himself "confronted by new challenges, surrounded by new acquaintances...I was suddenly seeing, feeling, and listening as a child sees, feels, and listens. It was one of those rare interludes that can never be repeated, a time of enchantment."

Writer Anne Morrow Lindbergh knew. "How wonderful are islands! Existence in the present gives island living an extreme vividness and purity. One lives like a child...in the immediacy of here and now."

E. B. White in Maine . . .

Lindbergh on an island . . .

We on a Maine island, through the tender memories of a child, found precious childness.

Eugenia said she and her brothers gave thanks for each beautiful sunset. We give thanks too, to both God and her — the One for providing the eventide miracle, the other for calling attention.

Children have that knack too, which adults often fail to recognize, dismissing recalled moments of childhood as simplistic and saccharine. Why should serious adults care?

Because: It is the child's sweet recollection that flavors the loving adult, and adults who define the world. Want a more loving world? Recapture childhood's sweet truths.

For just as adults are here to teach children, children are here to remind adults. What children know, adults used to know. We were born with the knowing. The knowledge we need is not so much to be *discovered* as *uncovered*. It is already inside. It's just that we have piled it over with unreal layers of life as we have been deluded to think life should be. It is smothered beneath an acronymic anarchy of CPA's and CPU's, MTV's and ATV's, VCR's, CFC's, IUD'S and HUM-V's; CEO's in BMW's doing LBO's; PR, the GOP, GQ and W, QB's, DH's, R-17's and W-2's. If ever we are to regain childness, we'll have to, like children, learn our alphabet.

Bracken fronds as parasols! What a delightful image for a girl to conceive and a woman remember.

It reminds us that the mind is kind. Memory clings to bliss and aggrandizes good, while veiling the bitter and mean. In pristine reflection, a child's life on an island was hot gingerbread and facefuls of violets because memory selects. That is the secret of "a happy childhood," or "the good old days."

But, of course, that's not enough. Selective memory can change only *then*. Many of us want to modify *now*.

Eugenia seemed to know how. Seemed to understand that the mind's beneficent power works as well in present tense as past. That to alter lives, we need to reframe attitudes. That as selective memory rewrites yesterday, selective perception can edit today.

When she says "*It was not always convenient to live on Bar Island,*" she is stating a fact, not complaining. Not grousing about wet feet nor access denied, but laughing at the boisterous splashing through incoming tide, or a loving uncle rowing to rescue. The pictures her reminiscences print on our minds are mirthful because her attitude was wilfully merry.

This, then, is the lesson which two who followed her draw from her pages, the thoughts they carry as they walk the paths she walked, hear whistling in winds through her popples, taste in her sun-warmed berries, and smell in the perfume of her aunt's spring lilacs. It is The Lesson of Bar Island and it is simple. As simple as a child's joy.

To the extent you choose each day to dwell on the sublime in life — life will be sublime.

Or, put another way:

Those fronds of green that spread at the foot of the oaks, if you think of them so, they are bracken — wild, inedible, useless. Or, if you wish, they are parasols. On an island, you always have that choice. And, one way or another, we all live on islands.

May you walk beneath parasols of fern.

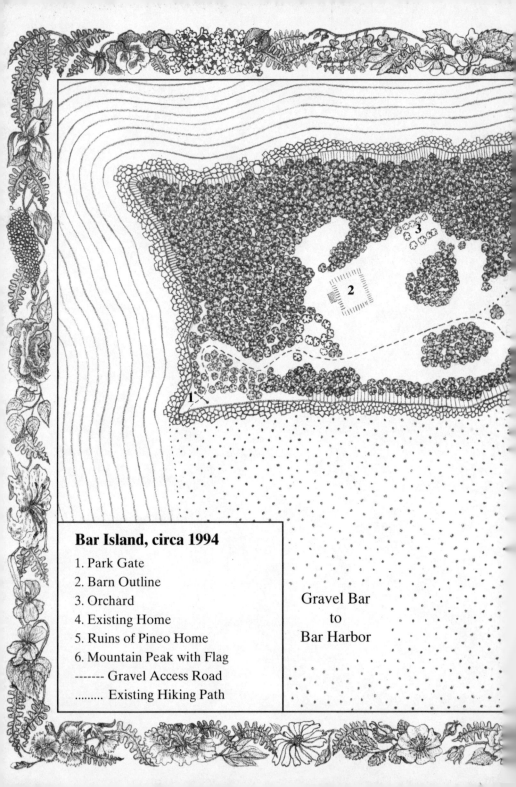

Bar Island, circa 1994

1. Park Gate
2. Barn Outline
3. Orchard
4. Existing Home
5. Ruins of Pineo Home
6. Mountain Peak with Flag
------- Gravel Access Road
.... Existing Hiking Path

Gravel Bar
to
Bar Harbor